Surf Avenue Girl

and other poems

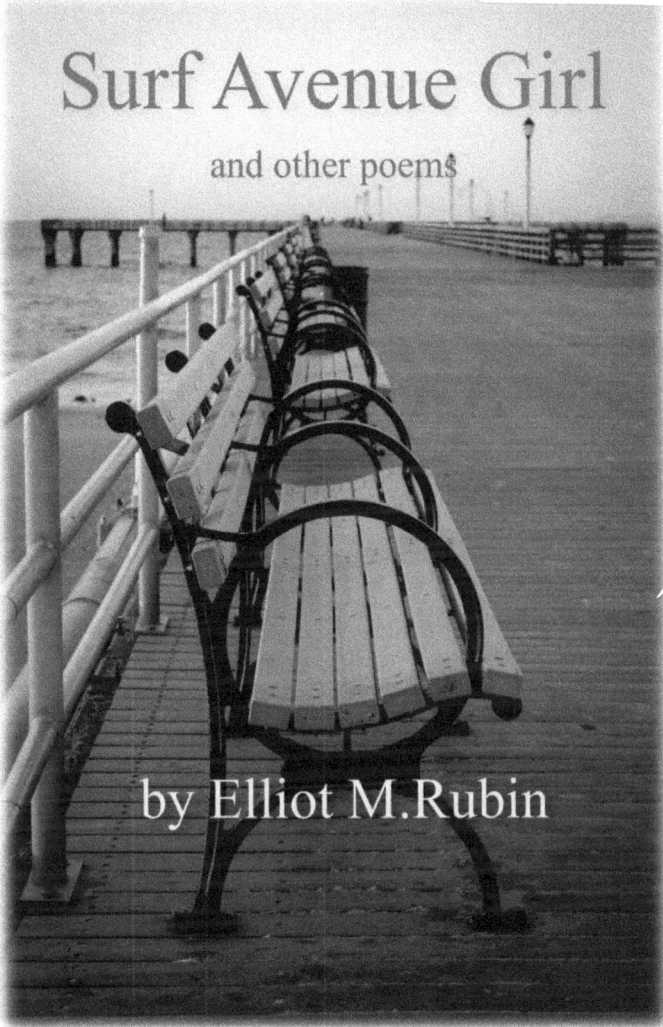

by Elliot M. Rubin

Surf

Avenue

Girl

And other poems

By Elliot M. Rubin

Preface

This book of poetry is about Brooklyn New York, and the people who live there. Most of it is specifically centered on the Coney Island section, but it covers the borough where I grew up and did business.

If I had not lived through many experiences as a young man I would not have been able to write this book of poems.

I believe poetry should be easy to read and understand. You do not need a college degree in literature to enjoy my poetry.

The stories are drawn on reality, and tell a human interest point of view.

Surf Avenue is a main street through Coney Island. With the beach a block or so away, and housing projects scattered around the area.

I hope you enjoy the book.

Dedication
To the many friends and acquaintances
from my youth who made this book possible.

In Memory of
Herman S. Rubin
Who wrote poetry all his life.

Table of Contents

Surf Avenue Girl

Surf Avenue, Brooklyn, in the eighties
is a rundown, fun-weary ghost
of its glorious past

with an empty carousel twirling 'round,
and its cacophony of music blasting out
the door, I could hear it as I drove by
on my way to work

the Coney Island of generations past
still lives in our memories, and
empty storefronts attest to the decay
of past frivolities

the early morning sun
forces the pretty Night Doves
to turn in for the day;
in their revealing spandex clothes,
sparkle makeup and teased hair,
handing over the cash
from their night's work
to their Peacocks, who are wearing fur coats
and sitting in gleaming Cadillacs,
watching them,
with music blasting into the early morning air

the Avenue ends under the Belt Parkway
across from Coney Island Hospital.
I stop at the traffic light,
witnessing a Night Dove getting beaten with a shovel
by a huge Peacock in the middle of the street

just another Surf Avenue Girl
living and working in Brooklyn

Party in the Projects

a group of guys got together one night
to hang out, and one of them decided
to call her for some fun

in the projects off Surf Avenue,
on the fourth floor, the phone rings and
she is convinced to invite all seven
of them over for a small party

her mother is out, somewhere unknown,
so there is no one home but her

he is invited up with his friends,
and most take turns with her that evening

the girl is a bubbly, chubby teenager
almost seventeen and lovelorn,
eager to please, to be adored
and to be wanted by the boys

but she is in love with one particular boy
because of what he did to her
that no one else ever dared

he kissed a Surf Avenue Girl
and she is now out of her mind crazy for him,
willing to do anything he asks

a young Brooklyn tough guy,
bravado is his shield,
so no one knows
he is as desperate as she is
for love
and affection.

Fishing under the Boardwalk

she placed her arms around his waist,
with tenderness
pulling them together;
he moves his lips closer to hers,
they kissed
under the creaking
Coney Island boardwalk

the lifeguards are off duty
the moon is not yet full,
lights from the arcade stands glisten
on the pounding surf
not so far away

people walking above look out
to see the fishing boats glide by,
dragging their nets behind, spread out,
trying to snag the catch of the day

they don't know the love below
is an everyday business transaction
spread out on the sun-drenched sand,
trying to snag her big catch of the day
as a hustling Surf Avenue Girl

Wasting Time

Surf Avenue is a busy street,
with drivers in their cars, hustling along
trying to find a parking spot
so they can run out
and grab a hot dog and drink
from Nathan's

in the evening, and early morning hours
the police keep traffic moving
or else cars would be triple-parked
backing things up for blocks,
making it hard
for the lustful to examine
the beautiful nighttime doves
walking along the avenue;
as cars cruise leisurely
windows down
calling out to find a dove
to party with tonight

the out of towners don't know
they can't sweet talk a Surf Avenue Girl;
"you wasting my time or what?"
is the retort they'll receive

time is money, and they don't waste it.
daylight is the end of their workday;
only so many hours to hustle
and so many men to entertain

Slice of Life

early morning she packed up her lunch,
made one for her young son,
then woke him
and laid out his clothes for school

almost time to leave for work
when the teenage girl next door
knocked to come in;
and take him to school
when he was dressed and ready to go,
with his house key on a string around his neck

her husband was killed two years ago
while working at a liquor store near
Surf Avenue; he gave them the
money, but they shot him anyway

life is not easy for her,
working three jobs from early morning
till almost midnight

she is lucky.
the Transit Authority
hired her to clean subway cars
in the Coney Island yards,
near the project she is living in.
then she works cleaning offices nearby
for cash after she punches out

no time for a real romance,
no time for almost anything.
she still owes
money for her husband's funeral
to a loan shark in the projects

he likes her, so he goes easy on
the payments. she worked out a
plan where she cleans his apartment
and gets a reduced rate

if he's home when she's cleaning,
she can reduce the payback even more
by being extra friendly to him

her responsibility is to her son,
and she does not forget him;
while living as best she can
as a Surf Avenue Girl

Lucky Surf Avenue Girl

walking downstairs to the lockers,
she quickly undresses and sprays
glitter all over her body

up the shadowy stairwell behind the
stage, she waited for the disk jockey to
start playing the songs to which she will
dance; the men throw money at her,
pawing and clawing for a touch, a feel

later, at the bar, she meets a young man
about her age, late teens or so; they
hit it off, and start to date hot and heavy

a few weeks later, he hit the largest
lottery jackpot
in state history

asked to move with him to the
southwest, she does.
but soon realizes
she doesn't love him,
returns the large engagement ring,
and moves back east to dance once more

not long after returning
another young man
enters her life,
moves in with her,
and he too wins a
multimillion-dollar jackpot

she leaves him
for the same reason

making a hundred grand
a year in cash while dancing,
she works selling furniture
to show legitimate earnings

the question many
people want answered,
is what talisman
did these guys
rub

for good luck?

The Newly Wed Groom

one summer night closing the store,
the lights are out,
the back door is locked,
the three of us are about to leave,
when a Surf Avenue Dove
walks by and looks in the window

she is young looking, about mid-twenties,
until the glare from the halogen street lights
revealed the rivers of lines on her face,
and the weariness in her eyes

she is slightly overweight,
with blown-out frizzy reddish hair
and unkempt clothes;
wearing an oversized baseball jacket
open in the front, with an unbuttoned blouse
exposing her braless chest,
and a large blue butterfly tattoo in the middle

the young salesman had come back
only last week from his honeymoon;
he waves and opens
the locked front door to talk to her

she offers him a tryst for ten dollars,
and he accepts.
they run downstairs to the basement
while we stand by the front door
for a few minutes,
waiting…
for the newlywed to reappear

She Smiled at Me

on the corner is an old
worn-out apartment house.
walking by one morning
on my way to work,
i noticed a tall, slim,
young blond Dove
shuffled slowly out of the building,
and stepped into a car
with four much older men

looking into the vehicle
i saw most of them wore
creepy, pencil-thin mustaches,
and furrowed lines
carved into their faces

these were not young men,
but older hardened guys,
who appeared to have a history
you really don't want to know

she looked up at me and smiled

i thought it a sad doe-like smile,
helpless, from the look in her eyes,
in a situation knowing

her immediate future,
as she squeezed
into the back seat
between them

then they drove away

The Birdcage Full of Doves

the elderly grocer next to my business,
after his wife died, gave food instead of money
to a Dove living in an apartment above his store
.

she is nothing to look at, and neither is he

the woman is a young divorcee
with two kids, living in a decrepit
four-story walk-up;
but everyone has needs, and they both decided
how to best meet theirs; a coincidence of needs

sometimes, he delivered around the block
to a one-family home on the corner;
it is a house of bill-and-coo,
where birds of a feather flock to pay

on any given late afternoon
as i walk to my car,
i see there are always three or four
black and white Doves
waiting on the sidewalk,
for the madam to let them in

on Saturday mornings about nine o'clock
when i arrive to go to work,
i turn off my car
across from their house, and
always notice the blinds alwaysflip up
their eyes peering down at me,
waiting to see if i walk
to their side door to enter

who knew Brooklyn is a birdcage full of Doves?

Prayers from Coney Island at Night

as the roller coaster reaches its zenith
overlooking all the buildings by the beach,
the riders raise their hands in the air
and feel like they're touching heaven

swoosh, the cars are racing downhill
while the air pushes back their faces;
teeth clenched shut and lips flapping
as they scream to God for help

though safe and secure strapped in,
the experience is new to many;
they hold onto the bar in front
while shrieking with excitement
and maybe fear

the lights in the distance are many,
as shadows stand out by default,
the prayers below are muted
as her muggers run away to escape

beaten and battered for no reason
as she went for a walk to relax,
she's lying in her own blood, crying,
as people walk past, looking up

A Perfect Day

there was bashing at her front door;
two large men were standing outside,
asking for him

she knew what they were looking for; their money;
his gambling debts had to be repaid, and he was gone

"he left me two days ago after we argued
and I have no idea where he went.
I don't even have enough money to buy food
for my two boys, or even gas for my car"

they could care less about her situation,
nor that in two days it will be Christmas

one of them said he wants her jewelry
and whatever else is of value in the apartment.
otherwise, they would take their revenge on her

when they left with her gold wedding band,
two gold chains, a television and other valuables,
the county marshal showed up to evict her

placing clothes in a few garbage bags
she threw them in the back of her car.
wearing jeans, and a torn tee-shirt,
she was forced to leave;
the officers did not help her pack

homeless with nowhere to go
and two boys, safely in school,
the Surf Avenue Girl
started driving in circles
trying to decide what to do

her parents had disowned her when she eloped;
somehow, they felt he was not right for her, or anyone
for that matter; so there is nowhere for her
to turn except, possibly, public assistance

desperate and hungry, she parked
by a convenience store
and went in to get a coffee

with her last few dollars
she bought one lottery scratch-off ticket,
then took out a coin to see if she'd won;
she didn't

with tears flowing down her cheeks, she stood
motionless in the middle of the store;
an older man, online for coffee, and wearing
a bespoke suit, noticed her in tears,
and asked if she was okay

depressed, she told him about her day
and the man listened intently

he said, "*Merry Christmas*"
and handed her an envelope;
then walked out with his coffee
with not another word

she tore open the small white envelope
and discovered it was a holiday card to his daughter

stuck inside the fold was five hundred dollars
speechless,

she watched as the stranger drove away

Coffee, Caffeine, and Bullets

the caffeine from the black coffee finally hit,
her eyes darting down the street
looking at oncoming cars;
hands shaking,
electricity coursing through her veins;
waiting is hard

her miniskirt exposed her rear
in a peekaboo style,
teasing the boys
cruising for a night of fun;
the chilled night air
with a cool breeze from the ocean
made goosebumps rise
on her naked arms and legs

the Surf Avenue Girl turns down offers from
the walk-bys, they have no money, not enough anyway
to make it worth her while

expensive cars are her style, her type, if you will,
clean cut with a Rolex on his wrist;
she is careful and highly discerning

finally, a big ass BMW rolls next to her,
and a darkened window glides down

"hey baby, want to party?"
a voice calls out to her

looking inside, she sees two men,
and likes their preppy look

"let me see your cash honey before I answer"

the car drives onto a side street
and stops next to the curb;
looking in she sees a hand with money
resting on the gear shift

without warning
she is pulled inside
through the open window,
going in headfirst,
with hands molesting her all over;
a life and death peril just began.

struggling, she reaches in her bag and
pulls out an illegal snub-nosed .38

the Surf Avenue Girl walks away
with the money,
leaving behind

a mystery for the cops

A Surf Avenue Showpiece

on a cruise, we always take the late dinner

this allows us to see a show every night,
lingering at the table talking
about something or other
with our six friends, our
constant traveling companions

one night i noticed a mature woman,
full-bodied but not fat,
in a tight-fitting, low cut, gold sequin dress
walking with a man considerably older,
who was using a cane to steady himself

his suit was loud, garish, and something a
hip hop or rap singer might wear;
not someone his age, who is only trying
to reclaim the appearance of youth

holding onto his arm
the woman grips it firmly to steady him;
i notice on her fingers, a slew of gold rings;
some with diamonds like doorknobs,
and she is fawning all over her husband

her long blond hair flows
with every step she takes
draped over her ample bust,
as he radiates happiness
to everyone he passes

i imagine he will die with a smile on his face

Forever Love

lying in bed
she backed her body against mine,
as my arm flung over
bringing her closer to me,
until we were cuddled as one,
closing our eyes to sleep
with smiles on our faces,
and loving the oneness
of a pair

we have done this for years
being together in love,
but we realized it was not for long
as her husband would soon be back

we met at school and dated. i
don't remember why we split;
but a reunion is a happy affair
and it continues when it can

we travel all over for business as
our spouses go to work all day;
we grew up in the projects
and swam at Coney Island

once you love a Surf Avenue Girl
she is in your life forever,
there is nothing much you can do
so don't resist the feeling

An Affair with a Surf Avenue Girl

standing next to her
looking out the window
at her husband mowing the lawn,
i suddenly feel
feminine fingers gently exploring, searching,
feeling their way to hold my hand
in hers

the soft touch of her skin,
the scent of her discount store cologne
floating from her body airmailed the message to me
of what she wanted, and intended to do

"at last, we are alone," she whispers in my ear

surprised, and not expecting this, i smiled,
chuckled a small nervous laugh,
and turned to face her

"Mom"
i heard her teenage daughter call from upstairs,
a momentary hitch in her plans, I thought…
a distraction

a few years later, she would be divorced
and a free woman on the prowl for lust,
eventually remarrying a richer man
then her current husband

today, though, i am the hunted,
her sought-after prey

over the years, i socialized with them both,
going to friend's house parties and other functions;

there is no way, I thought, I could
do what she has in mind

but how do I gracefully resist the temptation?

like a red sports car in the showroom,
imploring me to take a test drive
and then going home alone
without it,
wanting to come back for a spin

i am in a quandary.

Dancer in Walmart

standing in front of me on a checkout line
after she bought a toy shopping cart for a young child,
is this attractive Surf Avenue Girl, wearing
tight, black nylon spandex pants hugging
her very thin torso

a light fall jacket is unzipped
on a cool November day,
and her flashy multicolored blouse
is slit down the front
exposing the top of her full bosom,
supported by a push-up bra
for all to gaze upon;
like the sunrise peeking out
from the east at dawn

in full sparkle makeup, although
it is about noontime today,
her hair is fully teased,
and her sleazy looking boyfriend
is wearing a scruffy, soiled pullover
sweatshirt, waiting on the
next checkout line,
where he can buy his cigarettes

when I look at them
walking away together,
i want to tell her,
she
  aimed
    too

A Congressional Politician

i was standing in the doorway
of my business
on Coney Island Avenue,
looking out at the cars whizzing by,
when i saw across four lanes of traffic
on the other side of the street,
a homeless woman walking
trudging along,
and carrying in each hand
a bulging shopping bag full of what
I can't even begin to imagine

she was wearing a heavy
overcoat
on a warm spring day,
with boots, and a long skirt

she stopped

there are three four-family
homes on that side of the street

walking between two of them
she placed the bags down
on the walkway,
then squatted facing the avenue
and proceeded to relieve herself

with no propriety
or caring for others,
and only her self-interests and needs;
i thought she should be in Congress.

Family

school is annoying to her, so
the teenage Dove skipped classes,
to swim and sun at the beach
and fool around with the boys

her father likes to garden,
a retired sergeant from a local precinct;
who buried deep in his backyard
under the thick-thorned rose bushes,
his illegal bounty
beneath the beauty of the petals

the cash was earned the hard way
by Surf Avenue Doves at night;
he was a crooked cop
who shook down all the peacocks
and stole their drugs and money

the police raided the projects,
they found them full of young Doves,
and their Peacocks full of cash

the occupants were questioned
and all their money taken
before shipping them off to jail,
to await their fate in court

as they led them out of the precinct
one cop was surprised he saw a girl,
and recognized her right away;
his daughter had been arrested

he had stolen her hard-earned cash
and later buried it at home

she turned him in, out of anger,
but he escaped prosecution
by squealing on his buddies
so he could tend his roses
while they went away for years

the daughter went back to work
and they never spoke again;
she moved out and went independent
as a Surf Avenue Girl once more

Mary Felice

it is very early in the morning,
when Mary's mother wakes her to
send her off to school without breakfast

clients will be visiting soon, and she needs
the small apartment empty
without a kid in it

only ten years old
with tousled hair and rail-thin,
dressed in used clothes
bought from the local church's
consignment shop,
she ignores the small openings
on seams, or unsightly stains

dressing quickly and ushered out,
she starts off to go to school
by herself

hungry and bitterly cold
from the blowing wind coming off the water,
her light cotton sweater
does not keep her warm

a girlfriend down the block
tells her to stay in the lobby of her building,
and wait till she comes down
so she can go with her to school

she sits on a bottom step
in the stairwell,
the lobby is toasty warm, and
the weather outside is ungodly rough

they walk together every day,
and this morning is no different

tomorrow starts their Christmas break
as they pass a small neighborhood toy store,
they stop to look in the window

a bunch of dress-up dolls
is on display.
pretty costumes, hair flipped up
at the ends;
they couldn't stop staring and hoping,
maybe Santa will visit them
tomorrow night, and put one
under their tree

there is no tree in her home,
mom had to choose
between it and booze

in school, she receives a hot lunch
which will be her main meal of the day

this afternoon she stays late
hanging out
in the heated school, until dusk
when the janitor asks her to leave

arriving home,
she opens the door to her apartment
and walks in, praying tonight
Santa might visit her
with a dress-up doll

mom doesn't answer her shouts

walking into the bedroom,
she sees her mother
stretched out on the bed;
pills, and a half-empty
whiskey bottle
next to her motionless,
blue, naked body,
and a man's tie strangling her neck

the police soon come as does the medical examiner;
later, social services and the foster care people,
who take Mary Felice away,
never to return

in the tumult of the situation, nobody notices
sitting in the corner of the room
is an old, ragged bedroom chair,
piled high with worn, unwashed clothes

hidden behind the chair is an unwrapped box,
containing a new dress-up baby doll,
forever awaiting Santa's deliverance

Mamacita Carolina

uneducated, short, and here illegally,
she escaped her country
after the soldiers raped her
and shot her husband dead

alone, she worked two jobs to make ends meet.
she also nurtured the kids on her
block, feeding the hungry when they
had nothing to eat, and never saying no
to help someone in need

when she reached the big fifty, she fell ill,
and slowed down. the doctor told her
there is not much time, maybe weeks,
there is nothing he can do,
pancreatic cancer

depressed, she took the subway home

while walking up the steps to the street
a young hood shot her,
ran off with her pocketbook,
and left her lying on the dirty, cold
concrete steps to die

the homeless will miss her; the hungry will too.
she never remarried or had children of her own.
no relatives anyone knew of

at her funeral
            the line of mourners
                        stretched around the block.

Gowanus Canal

i was a teenager when my father
took me to a small upholsterer
near Brooklyn's polluted,
foul-smelling,
Gowanus Canal

under elevated tracks
in a dingy, always in shadow storefront,
was Sal's upholstery shop

he was a short, stocky, rotund man,
balding, with an air of swagger in his being;
suddenly my father stopped
dealing with him.

it turns out he was sitting in a bar, when
the cops said they walked by his white van
and saw stolen goods in the back

the problem is
there were no side or rear windows
on his van;
someone must've ratted him out

Sal said he had no idea how the
stuff got in his vehicle,
parked only a block or so from the canal

never heard from him again, till I
saw a car park across the street
from my store,
some ten years later

Sal exited and using two forearm crutches
hobbled in; he said hello to me
like a long lost buddy

it seems he fell on hard times
since someone kneecapped him

i guess the Gowanus Canal isn't the
the only thing in the neighborhood
that is dirty

Infidelity on Surf Avenue

the night he came home from work and told her,
it destroyed her world, her refuge from chaos,
the oneness of a couple now evaporated

standing over her,
expressionless,
a blank look on his face
emotionally devastated,
she slumped to the floor, looking up at him

"Why, why, I don't understand?
she said, crying hysterically through streaming tears

she'd worked with him as he built up his business.
working nights helping out,
doing whatever was needed

now he is successful, has many employees,
and is making piles of cash;;
he told her he wants to be free,
he found a younger love elsewhere

without any savings of her own,
she depended on him
for her wellbeing, her future, the comfort of knowing
he'd be there for her, and it all disappeared
in less than five seconds with an ultimatum

depression suddenly struck
knowing she had lost everything;
the abortion she'd had so she could
continue working, and building
his future, and now she has nothing… alone
her world came crashing down

going into the bedroom to pack his clothes
he did not notice her silently following him

in a rage,
she plunged a large steak knife
into his neck,
twisting,
churning,
and slicing
while cutting deep into his throat

the court ensured her security
for the remaining years of her life

Brooklyn High School Crush

she was very pretty with long brown hair
reaching all the way down her back.
sitting in front of me in high school
i dreamt of asking her on a date;
i never did, she only dated the football players
and other jocks,
i was intimidated.

when she walked down the hallway
all eyes focused on her,
she wore tight sweaters,
and knew she had the stuff we all
wanted, desired, but would never attain
in our high school years

i played it cool with her, maybe too cool

she never acknowledged me
until one day I was at lunch,
when she sat at my table with her girlfriends.
with nothing to lose, i ignored her and
started to joke around with her friends,
and she started to laugh out loud at my humor

finally, i made an impression on her;
turning to me she asked if i understood
the lesson in class. i started to explain it
when she asked if i could help her
after school with her homework

flashing through my mind was the song
"you belong to me tonight"
maybe wishing dreams come true does work,
…and maybe not

Obligations

after the fourth cup
of hot black coffee
on a cool fall night
near the ocean,
a Surf Avenue Girl
is beginning to feel alive

her senses are heightened
aware of all the goings-on
while spotting potential income,
her hands are beginning to shake

she can't stand still from her nerves
and begins to walk-in traffic,
her short skirt hiked up high
advertising precious goods for sale

this job is not her chosen profession;
at fifteen, her mother was murdered
and her dad was nowhere to be found,
while a younger sister is now her daughter
because of a promise to a dying mom

she quickly became an adult
with responsibilities for one so young,
working late to bring in the money
while tonight is her sweet sixteen

Brooklyn Divorce

Her marriage is over.
  He lied when he said
He would love and cherish her,
  Through good times and bad.
When the doctor said
she had cancer,
  He didn't offer any comfort,
Until his mom said, man up;
  So he listened to his mother.
The truth is she told you;
  He is her flesh and blood.
But she loves you more than him,
  The one she gave life years ago

She worked and contributed
  To their bank account,
Now he wants everything
  But her blood.
He refused to move out
  While she cooked and cleaned,
  as he sat snoozing on the couch,
While she washed all the family's clothes,
  He is such a waste of life

  Now she can tell him
Today she hired a lawyer,
And soon,
  he will be gone.
The lawyer said she'll get half,
  So tell him these final words,
As he walks out the door today,
  "Screw you asshole;
I'll see you in court!"

Coney Island Storm

the young children hid
under the table,
at a tender age
they know about guns

it must be from the apartment next door
they cried out in panic and dread,
as their mother sat calmly
drinking her coffee,
one long slow sip at a time

life in the area is dangerous
and their mother does try to protect them;
sometimes she just can't do it

because they know the odds,
snake eyes will roll up
every now and then,
hopefully…
not tonight

the sound they hear is thunder
and a storm is roaring off the beach,
as they snuggle under their covers
lulled to sleep by the sound of the rain

Wings

five-year-old Celeste has been
in and out of Coney Island Hospital
for many years,
battling cancer

the company who makes the only
cure for her type of disease
last month increased
the cost per dose
to over fourteen hundred dollars

she is on the fourth and
last protocol to cure her,
and it is not working
as well as it should

it is December and all the
local sports teams are visiting
the children's ward,
to spread holiday cheer, and give out gifts

Christmas is only a few days away

with no hair
and smiling as best she can,
in a hospital gown with tubes sticking out,
she sits patiently with her mom

she is a small Surf Avenue Girl
innocent to the ways of the world;
there are smiles when visitors say hello,
and she talks softly while clutching her
little cloth doll in her arms

when everyone finally leaves,
a nurse who is working with her stops
and sees her hugging her mom,
then overhears five years old
little Celeste
ask her mother
this important question

"after i die…
how long do i have to wait
till i get my wings"?

Beyond Her Control

sometimes there is not a damn thing
you can do about it

she realized this when stopped at a light
and two young thugs pointed a gun at her,
demanding she leave her car;
then drove away while she stood watching
in the middle of Surf Avenue

in broad daylight about noontime
nobody yelled out or called the police;
the cars behind her continued driving
after the traffic light changed to green,
whizzing past, ignoring a lady
standing in the middle of the street

she'd cashed her unemployment check,
she'd bought her groceries for the week
and stowed them securely in the trunk of the car;
now a family's hunger pains will begin to growl

for the next whole week, there is no food
and her kids will go hungry too,
their father is in Rikers Island
so he is of no help to them at all

she did nothing to cause this event,
carjackings will cause much pain;
when the car runs out of fuel
they'll strip it of what they can,
and move on to their next joyride
until they are caught, or shot, or killed

A Moment in Time

i can feel the soft flesh
of your back on my hand,
as it glides down
ever so slowly
on your body

the scent of your being
floats towards me,
in a tantalizing wisp
drawing my lips closer to yours

as you tilt your head
to meet mine,
your gentle fingers
touch the nape of my neck,
the tenderness of your spirit
and your love, a sparkling river,
flowing softly to my soul

at this moment
we are united,
for all eternity
into my memory,
into my emotions
never to be forgotten

the years will come and go,
and our bodies will inevitably change
but the love we share right now
is chiseled in time, forever

Aging at the Beach

all the buses and trains
end at the Coney Island stop;
if you are going to the beach
for a day of fun in the sun,
this is the place you want to be

the girls must cross Surf Avenue
to reach the water's edge,
while the ocean's waves
roll in, to crest
and splash them all

once their feet touch
the beach, and the
magic grains of sand,
they immediately stop aging
and look many years younger

the older the women are
who sun themselves all day,
the smaller their bathing suits become
until it reaches a useless point,
when no man's eye ever notices
nor is even able to see them

Hash Marks

she wears her stretch marks
as a badge of honor,
like a road map
of destinations traveled on her skin,
proof of being desired
and still a beauty in her mind;
her kids traipse behind
as she nears the ocean's edge

a two-piece cut so small
no one notices or cares about the marks,
but the old surgical stitches on her body
they tell a different story

she was a wild girl in her youth
one of whom tales are still told;
it was the knife fight
that almost killed her,
and touched off a riot
at her school

a sojourn on Rikers Island
with others just like her,
one day woke her up to reality,
and changed her manner
and her mind

the judge made her an offer,
join the army or go to jail;
the discipline worked wonders for her,
she did four years and got out,
went back to Coney Island
then married and settled down

Confusion in Brooklyn

at the dinner table one evening
the family sat and prayed,
for guidance at the voting booth
for tomorrow they will vote

the husband is Puerto Rican
he came here as a child,
his wife is from Guatemala
he met her while on a cruise

it took years of filing papers
and patience not many people have,
she is now an American citizen
and is ready to participate

although she is now here legally
her cousin and family are not.
he works seven days a week
and rarely sees his kids,
they are asleep when he gets home
and leaves before they awake

the big issue is immigration,
her concern is, for whom should she vote?
a man who will destroy a family?
or one who sees hard workers
trying to achieve the American Dream?

Blizzard off the Atlantic

the tracks in the snow echo her footsteps
as she pushes herself forward fighting the wind,
school is let out early, way too early,
for her mother to leave work
to safely bring her home

buses are slowly sliding,
skidding to a halt,
sometimes going sideways
down Surf Avenue at noon

its tracks are followed by blind drivers
unable to see because of the gale,
they feel safe in the ruts in the snow
made by trucks and buses ahead

a hat pulled down past her ears
and the jacket collar buttoned tight,
the storm is coming in off the ocean
a biting wind is pinching her face

finally safe in her apartment,
first time her latch key has been used,
kissed by the warmth of being home
she looks out the apartment's window
at people getting off the bus,
waiting for her mother
to finally step down,
and cross the street
to safely come home

Grief in Asher Levy Park

in the fall,
the field of wildflowers
shed their beauty,
cover the dirt
with colorful falling petals
as the cold wind
blows in from the east

sitting on a park bench
bundled against the breeze,
watching a dance of death
as the flowers make
ready for winter

only the tears
for her child
buried last year
outnumber the petals
dropping on the ground

Two Timed

waiting outside the high school,
for him to come out the side door
is getting on her nerves; where is he already?
she said to herself; classes ended ten minutes
ago, and she needs to go home very soon

also standing on the sidewalk
about ten feet away,
is another girl,
who is waiting for him too;
he does not realize what is in store for him
as he walks out with a smile

when two Surf Avenue Girls
are involved with the same guy,
nothing good is going to come of it;
walking over to greet him, the girls
meet at the same time, as he innocently
approaches the sidewalk

eyes flair open, and tempers silently
rise, as the two girls realize they
are being played by him, though
they never dated and only flirted,
their immediate thoughts
are dangerous and confused,
as to whom to attack first

before they can do anything,
the quarterback on the school's
team walks over,
and kisses the boy on the lips;
they walk away together
leaving the girls looking dumbstruck

A Final Act of Desperation

tired of just surviving cold winters, and
the hassle of life at the age of thirty-nine,
the decision was made; she needed to do
something drastic to end this chapter of her life

selling all her furniture and
stuff which she never used,
she withdrew whatever money
she'd saved,
and took the subway to the
Port Authority Bus Terminal

the Greyhound bus to Fort Lauderdale
was not too bad,
boring and tedious at times;
she loved looking out the window
at America. the towns and cities she'd read about
but never visited, and those she'd never heard of
excited her too; this was the great adventure
of her life, and she was taking it all in

arriving and tired, she stops in a coffee shop
downtown, and orders one of their all-day breakfasts

as she was drinking her coffee, a dapper senior citizen
asked if he could join her at the table; her Brooklyn
accent gave away where she was from, but so was he

after hours of talking, he asked if she would
like to stay at his place, he had a spare bedroom
after his wife died and was lonely for some company

the elevator opened to a private floor, on the
Penthouse level overlooking the ocean

sitting on his sofa, she told him her life story,
including her mother's murder;
and how she'd supported a younger sister
in foster care
by walking the streets all her life

as he listened respectfully, he was
touched by her words;,
he gave her a key to the apartment
then showed her to a bedroom
where she could stay for as long as she'd like

after dinner, he said he was going to sleep;
just before retiring to his room, he said
"Good night," Mary Felice,

A Powerful Storm

one day last year
the weather channel
reported a massive storm
is building over the Atlantic,
and is heading west to shore

the next evening
i walked to the boardwalk
and looked out to sea;
in the distance,
i saw black and grey storm clouds
swirling on the horizon,
doing a frantic dance over the ocean
while electric fingers strike out from above,
lighting the sky at dusk

there are no ships to be seen,
they are all safe and secure in port,
while the storm rages out there
and is heading right at me

an hour later, standing on the beach
the wind buffets
my face
a light drizzle is starting to fall,
and water is running down my neck,
soaking my shirt

the waves are racing to shore,
raging with fury as they breach the beach,
one after the other in a continuous assault

watching the surf crest
and crash down on land,

it's water trickling
onto the grains of sand
dissipating its strength;
reminds me of an elderly,
prosperous and powerful person,
who bulldozed their way through life
regardless of who was in the way;
and now is on the verge of entering eternity,
equal to every other grain of sand on the beach

the next year on the very same day,
i am sunning on the spot where i stood;
this time it is sweat
running down my neck, not rain;
and the storm, like the powerful, is forgotten

BONUS

"Secrets"

Secrets 1

waking up before her husband
she puts bacon on the skillet,
breaks two eggs with only one hand,
pushes the bread down in the toaster,
then grinds a batch of coffee beans
to make a fresh brew for him

after eating half the food
he leaves for work, with a see-you-later,
and no, thank you for making breakfast

after he walks out the door

she sits down in his chair
and finishes what he left,
then tidies up the apartment
before her friend visits, as usual,
every morning at nine oh five

living only one floor below
yet the first time they met
had been in the laundry room,
in the basement of the building

almost two years ago;
they had struck up a conversation
and a true friendship had begun

hearing a few quick knocks on the door,
her pulse races, opening the door, she smiles,
letting in a special friend, welcoming her
with a big hug, a tender kiss on the lips,
and her heart beating faster
filled with anticipation

Secrets 2

he was in his mid-forties,
bald and heavyset, rotund even,
with an outgoing personality
he made friends
everywhere his job took him

as an independent handyman,
he worked for businesses
and homeowners too,
but it was the residential work he did
which made his marriage fall apart

nobody knew he played
harmonica professionally,
until one day we walked out to his van
and he played a foot-long one for me;
he turned down a job with a harmonica group
they were on a national television show on
Sunday nights,
playing tunes on their harmonicas

then he placed the instrument in the van
and alternately began singing an opera in Italian;
he was very talented and sounded very good.

but his undoing was a job he did
for a young twenty-something
Surf Avenue girl

seduced, he moved in with her,
left his wife and teenage daughters,
and took an office job for a steady paycheck,
to help make ends meet at home

he discovered something at work
he really should not have found,
and reported it to the police

two weeks later, on a sunny afternoon
he was shot and killed
while walking on the street

it looked like a random act of violence
and nobody ever found out
it was not

Secrets 3

her mother drives her to the hospital
when the contractions start to come
too close

this is her first pregnancy,
and she appears to be very nervous,
not about the delivery
but what her father is going to say

being a thin girl
she hides her baby bump,
by wearing oversized, baggy clothing;
but now the ruse is over

her father is a highly biased man
always preaching
something-or-other form the Bible
to justify his outlandish views

as the nurses enter and leave
her mother holds her hand
giving her only daughter support
as best as she knows how

the mother hasn't told her husband;
she doesn't want to drive away her only daughter
and soo, her only grandchild, as well

the baby is delivered
an innocent to the world;
when the newborn is handed to the girl
it is then that baby's grandmother realizes,
why her daughter didn't tell her father;
the baby does not have their skin color

Secrets 4

as a religious girl
she would rather teach
in a parochial school
then a public one

the sight of a cross
hanging on the wall
in front of a class
gives her comfort

every morning
she and her mother
always go to church,
never missing a mass

being a heavy set
girl, although
caring and empathetic,
there are not many
dating opportunities
available to her

so on Wednesday nights
she drives from Brooklyn
to Long Island to visit
a monastery

there is a monk she pities;
he is alone with neither family nor friends

both of them look forward each week
to their brief time together;
they find it very comforting,
in a supportive familial way

The End

Other books by Elliot M. Rubin

A trilogy of crime/adventure novels
Hot Cash/Cold Bodies
Kara Bennet - Vengeance
Dead Girls Don't Die

Romance and Murder in Bensonhurst

Flash Fiction
People Stories in 600 Words
(as told by a raconteur)

Poetry
Scrambled Poems from My Heart
A Boutique Bouquet of Poems and Stories
Rumblings of an Old Man

Jewish Satire
The Phartick Chronicles

www.CreativeFiction.net

www.ingramcontent.com/pod-product-compliance
Lightning Source LLC
Chambersburg PA
CBHW070027110426
42741CB00034B/2671